# BOOK ANALYSIS

Written by Joe Burgis

# **Brideshead Revisited**
## by Evelyn Waugh

Bright
Summaries.com

**BOOK ANALYSIS**

# Shed new light on your favorite books with

# Bright≡Summaries.com

**www.brightsummaries.com**

| | |
|---|---|
| **EVELYN WAUGH** | **9** |
| ***BRIDESHEAD REVISITED*** | **13** |
| **SUMMARY** | **17** |

    The army and I
    Et in arcadia ego
    The long vacation
    Shadows closing round
    Callously wicked, wantonly cruel
    Julia
    Femme fatale
    A sign
    Brideshead revisited

| | |
|---|---|
| **CHARACTER STUDY** | **39** |

    Charles Ryder
    Sebastian Flyte
    Julia Flyte
    Lady Marchmain
    Anthony Blanche

| | |
|---|---|
| **ANALYSIS** | **45** |

    Divine grace
    A souvenir of the Second World War
    An unfamiliar world

| | |
|---|---|
| **FURTHER REFLECTION** | **53** |
| **FURTHER READING** | **57** |

# EVELYN WAUGH

## ENGLISH WRITER

- **Born in London in 1903.**
- **Died in Somerset in 1966.**
- **Notable works:**
  - *Decline and Fall* (1928), novel
  - *A Handful of Dust* (1934), novel
  - *Scoop* (1938), novel

Evelyn Waugh was an English novelist and journalist. He was educated at Lancing College, Sussex and later earned a third-class degree from Hertford College, Oxford. After working as a schoolmaster, briefly attending art school, taking carpentry lessons and attempting to drown himself only to be put off by a jellyfish, he published his first book, a biography of the artist Dante Gabriel Rossetti, in 1928, and his first novel, *Decline and Fall*, later that year. There followed a conversion to Roman Catholicism in 1930, a second marriage in 1937, the births of seven children, journeys in Africa and South America, stints in the Royal Marines, the Commandos and the

Special Service Brigade during the Second World War and the publication of 13 more novels and several works of non-fiction, before his death on Easter Sunday in 1966. Waugh is revered as one of English literature's finest prose stylists and fiercest satirists. His greatest novels are typically both hilarious and disturbing and chronicle the chaos, disillusionment and moral ambiguity of the years between the two World Wars.

# *BRIDESHEAD REVISITED*

## THE SACRED AND PROFANE MEMORIES OF CAPTAIN CHARLES RYDER

- **Genre:** novel
- **Reference edition:** Waugh, E. (2012) *Brideshead Revisited*. London: Penguin.
- **1st edition:** 1944
- **Themes:** Catholicism, war, nostalgia, aesthetics, social class

*Brideshead Revisited* was Evelyn Waugh's seventh novel. It was published in limited edition in 1944 and came out in a public edition in May 1945. One *New York Times* columnist, in his review of the novel, wrote that Waugh displayed "a genius for precision and clarity not surpassed by any novelist writing in English in his time" (*New York Times*, 1945).

It tells the story of Charles Ryder's relationship with the aristocratic Flyte family: first his friendship with the charming but doomed

Sebastian and later his love affair with the beautiful but thwarted Julia. Its themes are memory, religion, love and death. Its first readers, according to Waugh's biographer Christopher Sykes, were "ecstatic" (Sykes: 337).

Unique among Waugh's novels, *Brideshead Revisited* continues to captivate readers: for its sumptuous depiction of undergraduate life in the 1920s and its contentious portrayal of the social upheaval provoked by the Second World War, it is adored and debated in equal measure.

# SUMMARY

## THE ARMY AND I

At the age of 39, our narrator, Charles Ryder, finds himself stuck in England while the Second World War unfolds abroad, his early enthusiasm for the army waning with every botched set of orders and false promise of action. "We had been through it together, the Army and I, from the first importunate courtship until now, when nothing remained to us except the chill bonds of law and duty and custom" (p. 3). He dislikes his subordinates – in particular the businessman, Hooper – as well as his superiors – chiefly his zealous commanding officer. The battalion is ordered to move to new quarters, though no one holds out much hope that any real action is imminent. "I don't want *much* you know" says Hooper, "just enough to say I've been in it" (p. 9). Charles assures him that the move is just another "flap" (*ibid.*). And yet when his servant tells him the name of the new base, Charles is deeply moved: "he had spoken a name that was so familiar to me, a conjuror's name of such ancient power, that, at its mere sound, the phantoms of those haunted late years began to take flight" (pp. 12-13). Charles has returned to Brideshead.

## ET IN ARCADIA EGO

Over 20 years have passed since Charles' first sighting of Brideshead, a magnificent country house. He takes us back to the scene of that visit, "when the ditches were creamy with meadowsweet and the air heavy with all the scents of summer" (p. 17).

Charles and Sebastian Flyte borrow a car and drive from Oxford, where they are students, to visit Sebastian's family estate at Brideshead. On the way, he recalls, they stopped and "ate the strawberries and drank the wine – as Sebastian had promised, they were delicious together – and we lit fat, Turkish cigarettes and lay on our backs" (p. 19).

Pausing in his recollection of this first visit, Charles delves further still into the past, to tell us how he and Sebastian met. At the beginning of his time at Oxford, Charles lived a respectable life and associated with the academic types. Sebastian was a famous figure in the university – not least on account of his constant companion, a large teddy-bear called Aloysius. One night, Sebastian – drunk – vomited through the window of Charles' ground floor rooms. By way of an apology, Sebastian invited Charles to lunch. Several others of Sebastian's set also attended. There was heavy drinking and heavy eating. For Charles, it was the beginning of a new existence:

> "I went full of curiosity and the faint, unrecognized apprehension that here, at last, I should find that low door in the wall, which others, I knew, had found before me, which opened on an enclosed and enchanted garden, which was somewhere, not overlooked by any window, in the heart of the grey city." (pp. 25-26)

It was at this lunch that Charles first met Anthony Blanche, "the 'aesthete' par excellence, a byword of iniquity" (p. 27).

Back to Charles' first visit to Brideshead: he and Sebastian finish their strawberries and wine and cigarettes and drive on until, "half a mile distant, grey and gold amid a scene of boskage, shone the dome and columns of an old house" (p. 29).

No other members of Sebastian's family are at home – much to his apparent relief – but Nanny Hawkins, Sebastian's childhood nanny, is in her rooms. They talk with her, and Sebastian shows Charles some parts of the house before they return to Oxford. Charles is mesmerised by the experience.

Charles abandons respectability and launches himself into a hedonistic new life. "I *like* getting drunk at luncheon" he tells his cousin Jasper, a more senior student, whose criticism he invites: "You, my dear Charles, whether you realize it or not, have gone hook line and sinker into the *very worst set in the University*" (pp. 35-36). Charles is unmoved. Later, Charles is taken for dinner by Anthony Blanche. Anthony disparages Sebastian at great length ("of course, those that have charm don't really need brains", p. 45), as well as Sebastian's family: "such a *very sinister*" bunch, he insists (p. 46). We learn that Lord Marchmain, Sebastian's father, left Lady Marchmain and went to live in Italy with a mistress. As Catholics, they could not be divorced, and the scandal endures. Despite Anthony's best efforts, Charles remains loyal to Sebastian.

# THE LONG VACATION

Charles returns home for the summer vacation. "One of the problems of the vacation is money" Charles explains to his father (p. 56). "Oh, I shouldn't worry about a thing like that at your age" his father replies (*ibid.*). At this point, war is declared. Charles is marooned at home, outmanoeuvred by his father at every turn, until a telegram arrives from Sebastian: "*Gravely injured come at once*" (p. 65). Charles rushes to Brideshead to find that Sebastian's grave injury is a crack in a small bone in his ankle – so small it has no name. Sebastian's sister, Julia, is grateful to Charles for coming to take over as nurse. Julia departs, leaving the house entirely to the two friends. "I, at any rate" explains Charles, "believed myself very near heaven during those languid days at Brideshead" (p. 71). Between admiring the architecture, tasting the fine wines of the cellars and walking in the grounds, there is also some talk of Sebastian's Catholicism, which Charles, at this point, cannot fathom.

They are disturbed when Bridey, Sebastian's elder brother, and Cordelia, Sebastian's younger sister, return for an agricultural show. "All the family charm was in her smile" Charles says of Cordelia (p. 81). Sebastian is keen to get away, now that members of his family have appeared. He suggests that Charles come with him to Venice to see his father, Lord Marchmain.

Charles first impressions of Sebastian's father are of "a noble face, a controlled one [...] slightly sardonic, slightly voluptuous. He seemed in the prime of life" (p. 88). Lord Marchmain's mistress, Cara, surprises Charles. Associated as she is in his imagination with the scandal of Lord Marchmain's flight from England, Charles is taken aback by the "middle-aged, well-preserved, well-dressed, well-mannered woman" he meets (p. 90). Cara volunteers to show them round the city. For Charles, a nascent artist, it is an extraordinary experience – a stunning tour of "the immense splendours of the place" (p. 91).

At the end of their visit, Cara reveals certain things to Charles about the Flyte family, particularly Sebastian and Alex (Lord Marchmain): "He may not admit it to you. He may not admit it to himself; they are full of hate – hate of themselves. Alex and his family..." (p. 92). She explains that both Sebastian and Alex despise Lady Marchmain (Sebastian's mother, Alex's wife). "And how has she deserved all this hate? She has done nothing except to be loved by someone who was not a grown up [...] When people hate with all that energy, it is something in themselves they are hating" (p. 93). She warns that Sebastian will become an alcoholic unless something is done to help him.

Charles returns to his father's house, Sebastian to his family home in London.

## SHADOWS CLOSING ROUND

Back in Oxford, things are not as they once were. Anthony Blanche has been expelled and is sorely missed. A don, Mr Samgrass, has started to monitor Sebastian at Lady Marchmain's request. Julia visits Oxford and brings with her an admirer called Rex Mottram, a Canadian with political ambitions. Rex invites them all to a party in London, which they attend briefly, before Boy Mulcaster, a contemporary at Oxford, suggests going to Ma Mayfield's – an infamous bar and brothel. Later, Sebastian, Charles and Boy leave Ma Mayfield's with newly acquired companions.

Sebastian drives and crashes and everyone is arrested. This marks the beginning of Sebastian's rapid decline.

Rex manages to get the boys out of the cells, but charges are pressed against Sebastian. It is only thanks to Mr Samgrass generously testifying to Sebastian's promising academic career that he is not sent to prison.

When Charles visits Brideshead at Christmas, he finds Mr Samgrass is also invited, his influence expanding. Sebastian is increasingly unhappy and Charles, in growing closer to the rest of the Flyte family, only adds to this unhappiness: "I became part of the world which he sought to escape; I became one of the bonds which held him" (p. 117). His drinking gets heavier and heavier, until one evening, at Brideshead, its true extent is revealed in a "small but unforgettably painful incident" (p. 118). Sebastian has been drinking all day and claims to have a cold to avoid dinner. Charles tries to remove the whisky from Sebastian's room, but Sebastian catches him: "You're only a guest here – *my* guest. I drink what I want to in my own house" (p. 120). Charles dines with the rest of the family, but later Cordelia goes to check on Sebastian and announces he is drunk. Later still, Sebastian comes downstairs to apologise to Charles and humiliates himself in front of his family. The next day, after a talk with Sebastian's mother, Charles and Sebastian return to London. "Have you gone over to her side?" Sebastian asks. "No, I'm with you" says Charles (p. 128).

In Oxford, Charles reports that "the shadows were closing round Sebastian" (*ibid.*). Lady Marchmain comes to visit and has another little talk with Charles, who assures her Sebastian is not drinking too much. Soon afterwards, however, there is another drunken incident. Lady Marchmain insists that Sebastian will not live with Charles, as planned, but instead with Monseigneur Bell, a fellow Catholic. Sebastian, refusing this, is taken away, leaving Charles alone. "I'm the loneliest man in Oxford" he tells a once-close friend (p. 133). Charles decides to leave to train to be a painter in Paris. He receives a letter from Lady Marchmain, explaining that Sebastian will travel first to Venice, to see his father, then to the Levant in the company of Mr Samgrass. She hopes it will do him some good.

## CALLOUSLY WICKED, WANTONLY CRUEL

Brideshead, just after Christmas. Mr Samgrass is giving the family, and Charles – briefly back from Paris – a slideshow of photos taken during his and Sebastian's adventures in the Levant. Sebastian is conspicuous by his absence from almost all of them. Charles soon discovers that alcohol has been banned from the house and finds his friend in very low spirits. Eventually, Sebastian explains that he gave Mr Samgrass the slip during their travels, aided by Anthony Blanche, whom he met by chance in Constantinople. Though they were reunited briefly, Sebastian pulled the same trick again on their return to England, "to ensure a happy Christmas" (p. 146), during which no one knew where he was until he phoned to have his bill at his hotel paid.

A hunt is organised, and everyone is pleased when Sebastian announces he would like to join in. However, his intention is to lose the hunt at the first opportunity and ride to the nearest pub and drink until evening. The only obstacle is money. He asks Charles to help him, who refuses at first but soon yields.

While the hunt is out, Rex Mottram arrives at Brideshead with a present for Julia: "a small tortoise with Julia's initials set in diamonds in the living shell" (p. 153). Charles recalls this as "a memorable part of the evening, one of those needle-hooks of experience which catch the attention when much larger matters are at stake" (*ibid.*).

When Sebastian returns to the house at the end of the day, he is drunk and disgraces himself. The next day, Charles decides to leave early, knowing he can no longer be of any solace to his friend. While saying goodbye to Lady Marchmain, he admits it was he who gave Sebastian money. "I don't understand how we all liked you so much" she replies. "Did you hate us all the time? I don't understand how we deserved it" (p. 157).

Soon afterwards, Charles is surprised by Rex Mottram in Paris. Rex was taking Sebastian to Switzerland to see a specialist doctor, but Sebastian escaped once again. Charles confirms there has been no contact between them. Over a princely Parisian dinner, Rex explains to Charles that Lady Marchmain feels guilty about the way she treated him. He also reports that the Flyte family's finances are in bad shape, and that Lady Marchmain herself is seriously ill. Rex is on his way to see Lord Marchmain to ask for his blessing to marry Julia.

## JULIA

"It is time to speak of Julia" our narrator declares (p. 167). Charles interrupts his own recollections to tell us Julia's story.

Julia was introduced into society in the summer of 1923, which some said "was the most brilliant season since the war" (*ibid.*). She shone and attracted a great deal of attention, but "she knew that, in that little world within a world which she inhabited, there were certain grave disabilities from which she suffered" (p. 169). These were, chiefly, the scandal of her father and her Catholic faith. "Of the dozen or so rich and noble Catholic families, none at that time had an heir of the right age" (p. 170). This opened the door for Rex Mottram.

Being older, foreign, rich and ambitious, he was attractive to Julia. His star was rising in political circles and, although he was renowned for an ongoing affair with the infamous socialite Brenda Champion, he was determined to establish himself at the very top, which meant finding a suitably well-bred and wealthy wife. Julia eventually agreed to marry him. She rejected her Catholicism in order to continue seeing him and overrode Lady Marchmain's objections to the engagement. In order for there to be a magnificent wedding, Rex decided to become a Catholic. "'That's one thing your Church can do,' he said, 'put on a good show. You never saw anything to equal the cardinals'" (p. 178). He converted, with minimal sincerity. Right before the wedding was due to take place, Bridey delivered his "bombshell" (p. 182). Rex, Bridey discovered, had been married before, making a Catholic wedding impossible. "'Don't you realize, you poor sweet oaf,' said Julia, 'that you can't get married as a Catholic when you've another wife alive?'" (p. 183). Rex had not realised. Instead of calling the whole thing off – as Bridey and Lady Marchmain would have had it – Julia and Rex married quietly, in a ceremony described by Julia as "squalid" (p. 185).

## FEMME FATALE

We rejoin the narrative in 1926, with Charles returning to England from France fearing that revolution is imminent. The General Strike is in full flow, and Charles volunteers with Boy Mulcaster to help do the jobs vacated by the strikers. Charles is invited to a party, where he is reunited with Anthony Blanche. Later, Julia invites him to Marchmain House (the Flytes' London home), where Lady Marchmain is dying. Julia asks Charles to try and find Sebastian, so he might see her before she dies. Charles agrees.

He travels to Fez, Morocco, where the British Consul gives him news of Sebastian. "I *like* Flyte [...] He was always perfectly charming, and my wife took a great fancy to him" (p. 196). When Charles arrives at Sebastian's house, he finds only a German called Kurt, nursing a toe he tried to shoot off to escape military service, drinking beer and listening to jazz. Kurt explains that Sebastian is sick and in the hospital. Charles finds that he is "more emaciated than ever; drink, which made others fat and red, seemed to wither Sebastian" (p. 200). He is being looked after by monks. On hearing the news about his mother, Sebastian laments: "Poor mummy. She really was a *femme fatale*, wasn't she? She killed at a touch" (p. 201). Sebastian will not leave – he insists he must look after Kurt – and in any case he is not well enough to travel. Lady Marchmain dies while Charles is with him. He sees Sebastian safely home, then returns to London.

Marchmain House is going to be sold and knocked down to alleviate the Flytes' financial difficulties. Charles is commissioned by Bridey to paint four pictures of the interiors. The project is a great success, and launches Charles' career as an architectural painter: "I could do nothing wrong [...] Bit by bit, minute by minute, the thing came into being [...] each brush stroke, as soon as it was complete, seemed to have been there always" (p. 204).

## THE END OF THE DEAD YEARS

> "For nearly ten dead years [...] I was borne along a road outwardly full of change and incident, but never during that time, except sometimes in my painting – and that at longer and longer intervals – did I come alive as I had been during the time of my friendship with Sebastian." (p. 211)

Charles finds success as an architectural painter. He marries the glamourous Celia, Boy Mulcaster's sister. Then, having found out Celia was conducting an affair, he travels to Central and South America to paint wilder pictures.

He is reunited with Celia in New York. "In Europe," he reflects, "my wife was sometimes taken for an American because of her dapper and jaunty way of dressing and the curiously hygienic quality of her prettiness" (pp. 213-214).

On board the liner from New York to England, Charles meets Julia. During an immense storm, which consigns most of the passengers, including Celia, to their beds, Charles and Julia begin their affair. "In that minute, with her lips to my ear and her breath warm in the salt wind, Julia said, though I had not spoken, 'Yes, now,' and as the ship righted herself and for the moment ran into calmer waters, Julia led me below" (p. 243).

They agree to meet in London.

Charles exhibits his pictures. Anthony Blanche attends and afterwards and takes Charles for a drink. Of Charles' exhibition, he says:

> "I found, my dear, a very naughty and very successful practical joke. It reminded me of dear Sebastian when he liked so much to dress up in false whiskers. It was charm again, my dear, simple, creamy English charm, playing tigers [...] Charm is the great English blight. It does not exist outside these damp islands. It spots and kills everything it touches. It kills love; it kills art; I greatly fear, my dear Charles, it has killed *you*." (p. 254)

Charles says goodbye to Anthony and meets Julia on the train to Brideshead.

## A SIGN

Two years later, Charles and Julia are sitting together by the fountain in the grounds at Brideshead. Both are awaiting divorces so they can marry each other. They are happy, but impatient. "'Sometimes,' said Julia, 'I feel the past and the future pressing so hard on either side that there's no room for the present at all'" (p. 261).

Later that evening, Bridey announces he is finally getting married, to a Mrs Muspratt. Julia and Charles are happy for him, until Bridey says: "'I couldn't ask her here [...] Beryl is a woman of strict Catholic principle [...] It is a matter of indifference whether you choose to live in sin with Rex or Charles or both [...] but in no case would Beryl consent to be your guest'" (p. 257). Julia – to Charles' great surprise – is deeply hurt by this. She and Charles argue. Charles understands that some fundamental impediment to their happiness is being revealed.

Charles gets his divorce from Celia. Julia's is delayed by Rex, who wants to wait, as his political reputation is fragile. Cordelia returns to Brideshead from Spain, where she has been working as a nurse. Julia describes her as "quite plain" (p. 281) and at first Charles agrees. But later: "As we sat there talking, and I saw Cordelia's fond eyes on all of us, I began to realize that she, too, had a beauty of her own" (p. 238).

Cordelia says she has visited Sebastian. He is living in a monastery, is popular with the monks, and still drinks. She envisages that he will carry on like this until one day in the not too distant future, having drunk too much, he will die. His companion, Kurt, was drafted into the German army, deserted, was captured and taken to a concentration camp, and committed suicide.

Lord Marchmain announces that he intends to return to Brideshead to live out his final years. When he arrives, it is clear he is unwell. "Julia gave a little sigh of surprise and touched my hand. We had seen him nine months ago at Monte Carlo, when he had been an upright and stately figure, little changed from when I first met him in Venice. Now he was an old man" (p. 295).

As Lord Marchmain's health declines, the question of having a priest attend him at his death arises. Lord Marchmain had rejected his faith vehemently, and Charles argues repeatedly that it would be an insult to thrust religion on him now, in his weakness. But Bridey and Cordelia disagree, and even Julia wavers. Bridey takes the decision to invite Father Mackay to the house, but the visit is a disaster. "Father Mackay, I am afraid you have been brought here under a misapprehension. I am not *in extremis*, and I have not been a practising member of your Church for twenty-five years. Brideshead, show Father Mackay the way out" (p. 307). The argument continues, until Lord Marchmain's death is imminent. It is Julia who takes the final decision to invite Father Mackay once more. Everybody watches as the priest administers the last rites to the dying man. And finally, even Charles is moved: "I suddenly felt the longing for a sign, if only of courtesy, if only for the sake of the woman I loved, who knelt in front of me, praying, I knew, for a sign" (p. 317). And a sign soon comes:

> "Lord Marchmain moved his hand to his forehead...the hand moved slowly down to his breast, then to his shoulder, and Lord Marchmain made the sign of the cross. Then I knew the sign I had asked for was not a little thing, not a passing nod of recognition." (*ibid.*)

It is the end for Charles and Julia. Julia realises she is unable "to set up a rival good to God's. Why should I be allowed to understand that, and not you, Charles?" (p. 319).

"I don't want to make it easier for you," Charles replies, "I hope your heart may break; but I do understand" (*ibid.*).

## BRIDESHEAD REVISITED

Charles receives his orders from his commanding officer, then goes to look round the house. He finds Nanny Hawkins is still living there, and they talk. He discovers that Julia and Cordelia have volunteered for the war effort somewhere abroad. Parts of the house have been vandalized. Rex Mottram is enjoying political success. Finally, Charles visits the chapel built by Lord Marchmain for his wife:

> "Something quite remote from anything the builders intended, has come out of their work, and out of the fierce little human tragedy in which I played; something none of us thought about at the time; a small red flame – a beaten-copper lamp of deplorable design relit before the beaten-copper doors of a tabernacle [...] It could not have been lit but for the builders and the tragedians, and there I found it this morning, burning anew among the old stones." (p. 325)

# **CHARACTER STUDY**

## CHARLES RYDER

Charles Ryder is the novel's narrator, described by Waugh's biographer Christopher Sykes as "far from loveable" (Sykes: 349). He is an oddly distant figure, passive and remote. Charles meets Sebastian Flyte at university and is briefly thrust into a world of aristocratic splendour – a world that, but for the chance of his having ground floor rooms at Oxford, through which Sebastian drunkenly vomits, he most probably would never have known. It is Charles we follow through "that low door in the wall" (p. 25) into this world, and through whose memories we experience its delights and its travesties. His relationship with the Flyte family culminates in his falling in love with the beautiful Julia, only for that love to be thwarted by the deeper claims made on her by her religion.

# SEBASTIAN FLYTE

Sebastian Flyte is the son of Lord and Lady Marchmain. At Oxford he is renowned for his wealth, good looks and charm. "The most remarkable invention of the book is without doubt Sebastian" Sykes writes, continuing:

> "Evelyn here achieved the very difficult feat of conveying the glamour of youth and privileged position without any recourse to romanticizing [...] of all Evelyn's many invented characters, Sebastian is the most successful, and indeed a perfect piece of drawing and painting. For that reason the description of Sebastian's decay is intensely moving." (Sykes: 347)

It is a tragic decline: plagued by demons, he becomes a drunk; he flees his family and friends; he lives in squalid foreign places and grows sicker and sicker. "One can have no idea", says Cordelia of Sebastian's suffering, "what the suffering may be, to be maimed as he is – no dignity, no power of will. No one is ever holy without suffering" (p. 326).

# JULIA FLYTE

Julia is Sebastian's sister. From the moment she is introduced into society, she is held to be glamorous and beautiful. She falls for Rex Mottram, a wealthy and politically ambitious Canadian, and marries him, despite the objections of her mother Lady Marchmain, and in doing so rejects, for the time being, her Catholicism. Later, she and Charles fall in love and determine to marry each other. But at the death of her father, Lord Marchmain, and after having witnessed the apparent resumption of his faith in the last moments of his life, Julia understands that she and Charles cannot be together. They separate. Critics seem to be united in their feeling that Julia, as a fictional creation, is deeply flawed. Sykes writes,

> "She never comes to life [...] Evelyn brought every device he could think of to make her vital and irresistible [...] But to no avail. The result is a carefully modelled wax mannequin. One may admire the beauty, the glamour and the modelling, but she remains a wax-work. Perhaps Evelyn tried too hard. Perhaps he failed with this central character because he was not drawing in the life-class; no one has yet discerned or suggested a model for Julia." (Sykes: 348-349)

## LADY MARCHMAIN

At once a saintly and poisonous presence, Lady Marchmain is both victim and villain. Scandalously abandoned by Lord Marchmain, she is determined to prevent history repeating itself. Her son Sebastian, like his father before him, turns to drink to help him overcome his demons. The more control she attempts to exercise control over him, the more he craves freedom. She recruits the obsequious Mr Samgrass to watch over him and she forbids Sebastian from living with Charles in Oxford. She is despised by Lord Marchmain and Sebastian alike for her pious accommodation of their failings. "I can think of no other writer" Sykes says, "who has presented so convincing a picture of the kindly mother-figure [...] who, with the best and kindest intentions, exerts a lethal stronghold on all around her" (Sykes: 347).

## ANTHONY BLANCHE

Anthony Blanche is the novel's most colourful, egregious, exuberant character. Charles tells us about his childhood:

> "Criss-cross about the world he travelled [...] waxing in wickedness like a Hogarthian page boy [...] there was a bluster and a zest in Anthony which the rest of us had shed somewhere in our more leisured adolescence [...] He was cruel too, in the wanton, insect-maiming manner of the very young, and fearless like a little boy." (pp. 39-40)

Anthony is a friend of Sebastian's and later Charles' at Oxford. He flits in and out of the narrative. Perhaps his most memorable performance is his last in the novel, during which he lectures Charles on the toxic nature of English charm: "It does not exist outside these damp islands. It spots and kills everything it touches. It kills love; it kills art; I greatly fear, my dear Charles, it has killed *you*" (p. 254). Anthony Blanche was based on a friend of Waugh's, Harold Acton, who, according to Sykes, "was understandably hurt by this caricature drawn by one of his oldest and closest friends" (Sykes: 346).

# ANALYSIS

## DIVINE GRACE

In his preface of 1959, Waugh described the theme of *Brideshead Revisited* as being "the operation of divine grace on a group of diverse but closely connected characters" (p. ix).

Sykes elaborates:

> "The essential subject of the book was not youthful irresponsibility, youthful and mature love, the pageant of fashion, the splendour of aristocratic society, but certain Last Things: how to face death, the Christian Truths, the world-wide claims of the Catholic Church." (Sykes: 337)

It is unquestionably a Catholic novel. Its narrator, Charles, is a religious sceptic. For the sake of good manners he declares himself an agnostic, but his doubts run deep: "It seems to me" he says to Bridey of Sebastian, "that without your religion Sebastian would have the chance to be a happy and healthy man" (p. 133). It is only at the very end of his relationship with the Flytes that Charles feels the first stirrings of faith: as Lord Marchmain, close to death, makes the sign of the cross, Charles recalls, "Then I knew that the sign I had asked for was not a little thing, not a passing nod of recognition, and a phrase came back to me from my childhood of the veil of the temple being rent from top to bottom" (p. 317). When Charles returns to Brideshead with the army, years after all but one of its former inhabitants have either fled or died, after the world it once embodied has vanished and after war has overhauled the old order of things, it is only the "small red flame" burning in the chapel that endures (p. 326).

Waugh's theme was not one that novelists of the time commonly explored. "Evelyn was doing something" Sykes writes, "which seemed in England to have gone out of fashion forever; he was making religion the central point of a story about contemporary English life, and approaching his theme with respect and awe" (Sykes: 338).

Cordelia says of her father's faith: "Pompous, you know. It takes people in different ways" (p. 206). She explains to Charles that Sebastian's holiness is his essential quality: "Oh yes, Charles, that's what you've got to understand about Sebastian" (p. 286). Bridey's faith is matter-of-fact and Julia's is intermittent; Rex Mottram's is entirely artificial; Lady Marchmain's formidable, almost insufferable. For the novel's central figures, at least, character and religious sensibility are deeply intertwined.

## A SOUVENIR OF THE SECOND WORLD WAR

"My theme is memory, that winged host that soared about me one grey morning of war-time" (p. 211). So Charles elucidates his project.

*Brideshead Revisited* oozes nostalgia. It pines for former glories. In his preface, Waugh describes the conditions in which the novel was written:

> "It was a bleak period of present privation and threatening disaster – the period of soya beans and Basic English – and in consequence the book is infused with a kind of gluttony, for food and wine, for the splendours of the recent past, and for rhetorical and ornamental language, which now with a full stomach I find distasteful." (p. ix)

Sykes concurs with Waugh's assessment of the times. He explains why the novel had such an impact on its readers:

> "It was [...] an age of disillusion, of shortening rations, increasing discomfort and more and more an all-pervading shabbiness. Into this drab world there flashed for the happy few this immense entertainment, with its colour, its appeal to nostalgia stronger than at most times, its wit [...] abounding with what the world was most short of, fun." (Sykes: 337)

The most gluttonous scenes – like that of Charles' first lunch with Sebastian, at which plovers' eggs, lobster Newburg and Cointreau are plenteous – and the plushest sentences are reserved for Charles and Sebastian's university days:

> "Oxford, in those days, was still a city of aquatint [...] her autumnal mists, her grey springtime, and the rare glory of her summer days – such as that day – when the chestnut was in flower and the bells rang out high and clear over her gables and cupolas, exhaled the soft airs of centuries of youth." (p. 17)

Such richness of language simultaneously appealed to readers weary of the drabness of the times and invited the criticism of reviewers who dismissed it as indulgent. "They were dismayed by the lushness and sentimentality of much of the writing" Sykes explains (Sykes: 339). Waugh took some of this criticism on board; in the preface, he admits that he has "modified the grosser passages" but has not "obliterated them because they are an essential part of the book" (p. ix). The novel's admirers far outnumbered its critics.

## AN UNFAMILIAR WORLD

Sykes describes how the novel was received:

> "The reception of the book on the issue of the first edition was so enthusiastic that one can almost use the word ecstatic with precision. It came mostly from friends, it is true, but these friends contained a considerable proportion of people with claims to high and inalienable critical standards, Henry Yorke, Graham Greene, Desmond MacCarthy, Osbert Sitwell and John Betjeman." (Sykes: 337)

*Brideshead Revisited* remains Waugh's most widely-read novel. And Sykes makes the case for its enduring influence over later writers:

> "Since 1944 several writers, including Graham Greene, have attempted serious unsceptical treatment of orthodox Christian religion in novels, notably Iris Murdoch among Anglicans in The Bell. I think they all owe rather more to the example of Evelyn's novel than is commonly recognized." (Sykes: 338)

Waugh, rather forlornly, wrote that the novel "lost me such esteem as I once enjoyed among my contemporaries and led me into an unfamiliar world of fan-mail and press photographers" (p. ix).

# FURTHER REFLECTION

## SOME QUESTIONS TO THINK ABOUT...

- Waugh's critics accused him of snobbery in his depiction of Hooper. Do you agree with them? Why?
- How does the predominant theme of memory affect the style and structure of the novel?
- Can you think of other novels that are principally concerned with religion? How do they compare to *Brideshead Revisited*?
- Do you find the more luxurious prose appealing or off-putting? Why?
- How does *Brideshead Revisited* compare to other notable works of war literature?
- Do you agree with Christopher Sykes that Julia never really comes to life as a character? Why might this be?
- The novel describes a period that most modern readers have never known. Why do you think it continues to be so popular?
- How does *Brideshead Revisited* compare to Waugh's earlier novels?

*We want to hear from you!
Leave a comment on your online library
and share your favourite books on social media!*

# FURTHER READING

## REFERENCE EDITION

- Waugh, E. (2012) *Brideshead Revisited*. London: Penguin.

## REFERENCE STUDIES

- Hutchens, J. K. (1945) Evelyn Waugh's Finest Novel. *The New York Times*. [Online]. [Accessed 25 November 2018].
  Available from: <http://movies2.nytimes.com/books/97/05/04/reviews/waugh-brideshead.html>
- Sykes, C. (1975) *Evelyn Waugh: A Biography*. London: Penguin Books.

## ADDITIONAL SOURCES

- Stannard, M. (1990) *Evelyn Waugh: The Early Years, 1903-1939*. London: W. W. Norton & Company.
- Waugh, E. Davie, M. ed. (1979) *The Diaries of Evelyn Waugh: 1911-1965*. London: Penguin Books.

## ADAPTATIONS

- *Brideshead Revisited.* (1981) [TV Series]. Charles Sturridge. Dir. UK: ITV Studios Home Entertainment.
- *Brideshead Revisited.* (2008) [Film]. Julian Jarrold. Dir. UK: 2 Entertain.

# Bright≡Summaries.com

## More guides to rediscover your love of literature

- **Animal Farm** by George Orwell
- **The Stranger** by Albert Camus
- **Harry Potter and the Sorcerer's Stone** by J.K. Rowling
- **The Silence of the Sea** by Vercors
- **Antigone** by Jean Anouilh
- **The Flowers of Evil** by Baudelaire

www.brightsummaries.com

Although the editor makes every effort to verify the accuracy of the information published, BrightSummaries.com accepts no responsibility for the content of this book.

**© BrightSummaries.com, 2019. All rights reserved.**

www.brightsummaries.com

Ebook EAN: 9782808016193

Paperback EAN: 9782808016209

Legal Deposit: D/2018/12603/570

Cover: © Primento

Digital conception by Primento, the digital partner of publishers.

Printed in Great Britain
by Amazon